MAKING

COUNTRY WINES,

ALES & CORDIALS

by

BRIAN P. TUCKER.

Published by The Good Life Press Ltd., 2009
Reprinted 2011

ISBN 978 1 90487 1620
A catalogue record for this book is available from the British Library.

Published by
The Good Life Press Ltd.
The Old Pigsties
Clifton Fields
Lytham Road
Preston
PR4 0XG

www.goodlifepress.co.uk
www.homefarmer.co.uk

Set by The Good Life Press Ltd.
Printed and bound in Great Britain

CONTENTS

Soft Drinks Pages 7 - 14

Beer Pages 16 - 28

Wine Pages 29 - 72

Making Country Wines, Ales & Cordials

Introduction

Before we start out on the brewing process there are several things that need to be considered. Firstly, most of the drinks listed here are far too strong to be consumed by children, with perhaps the exception of some of the simpler drinks such as lemonade and the milder recipes of ginger beer, which include the sweet, still and dry sparkling versions. These are certainly suitable for any younger members of the party.

That said, let us now turn to more important issues such as actually begining to make the delicious wines, beers and spirits contained in this little book. Probably the most important fact to remember is that everything that is used in making the drinks, including even the little teaspoon used to either measure or mix the ingredients, must be spotlessly clean with not even a speck of dust anywhere in sight, and all fermenting vessels should be thoroughly sterilised. I shall keep on about this cleaning bit, but I can assure you that it is in your own best interests: you are embarking on what is, in effect, an experiment in chemistry and both the quality of your product and your health are of paramount importance!

The next point to make is that the recipes should be followed carefully and with no additions of any kind. You will notice too that many of the recipes need quite a long time to mature, even after the end of the brewing process, so you must take this into consideration when planing a party or even just a booze up, because if any of these slow maturing drinks are opened before the appropiate time the taste will, let me assure you, be a severe disappointment compared to the well-conditioned bottle of the wine you were probably expecting.

Having decided on your recipe, do make sure that you have all the necessary ingredients to hand and ready to use. It will make the task so much easier!

My original interest lay in making ginger beer and lemonade, but from there I progressed to making the bigger and stronger beers and drinks. I learnt most of these recipes from my father-in-law who taught me the fundamentals of making country drinks which he in turn had learnt from his mother, who had brought him up 'on the blanket,' as they say. He was part Gypsy.

I just hope that brewing these drinks gives you as good a time as I have had during my lifetime of both making and drinking these very fine wines and beers, and I wish you the best of luck in both making and enjoying them. But beware - on the whole they are considerably stronger than pub drinks and, although I wish in no way to be a party pooper or spoil sport, do use your common sense when consuming them.

Now that I have got all that off my chest let's get brewing - and have yourselves a great party!

Happy Brewing and Drinking!

Brian P. Tucker,
Devon 2009

Lemonade

8 large lemons
8oz caster sugar
4 pints boiling water

Wash and dry the lemons, then peel them very thinly using a potato peeler. Squeeze the juice from the lemons and place it in a covered plastic container in the refrigerator. Place the peel in a large jug or bowl with the sugar and pour over the boiling water. Stir briskly and cover before leaving in a cool place overnight. Next day pour in the lemon juice, strain in to jugs and chill. This will make approximately sixteen glasses.

Citrus Squash

This fruity squash is diluted with still or sparkling water so a little goes a long way.

2 large lemons
2 limes
2 large oranges
12oz golden caster sugar.
7fl oz water

Scrub the fruits well in hot water to remove any wax coating. Grate the fruit rinds finely and squeeze the juices from the fruit. Place the grated rinds and the sugar into a saucepan with the water and gently heat until all the sugar has dissolved. Boil for two minutes and then allow to cool. Stir in the fruit juices, strain the mixture into a jug and chill until needed. Dilute to serve.

This cordial can also be bottled.

Raspbery Fizz

1lb fresh raspberries.
3oz golden caster sugar
1 pint sparkling mineral water

Blend the raspberries with the sugar in a blender to make a puree.   Sieve the puree to remove all the seeds and pour into a jug. Add the sparkling water (or sparkling Wine for adults) and pour into ice- filled glases.

Elderflower Cordial

1½lb granulated sugar
1 pint water
1 lemon
12 elderflower heads

Place the water, sugar and grated lemon rind into a saucepan and heat slowly to dissolve the sugar. Remove the florets from the elderflowers and stir them into the sugar sryup. Leave the mixture to cool down and add the lemon juice. Strain the mixture through muslin and bottle.

To make the cordial up into a drink pour a tablespoon full into a glass and top up with ice-cold water. If the cordial is too sweet for yourc tastes, you can dilute it further with more iced water or add a drop of lemon juice.

This cordial will keep for up to six months in the refrigerator.

Ginger Beer

18oz sugar, preferably caster sugar
2 level tbsp ground ginger
2 level tbsp dried baking yeast
Juice of two lemons
16 pints water

Dissolve the sugar in a little of the water and clean out a plastic bucket. Sterilise it with Milton sterilising solution and rinse it very thoroughly. Place the rest of the water in the bucket and add the ginger, yeast, lemon juice and the sugar solution and stir. Cover the bucket and leave it to stand in a warm place to ferment for one week. After one week make sure that all the bottles and stoppers are ready for use by sterilising them, making sure to rinse them out well. Bottle the ginger beer using either a jug or a siphon tube and leave as much of the sediment behind as possible. Add one half teaspoon of sugar per pint, seal lightly and leave it to stand for at least one more week. The ginger beer will then be ready to drink.

Ginger Beer #2

GINGER BEER: two different drinks from a ginger beer plant.

½ oz general purpose dried yeast
½ pint water
Sugar
Ground ginger
Juice of two lemons

Place the yeast in a jar, add the water and 2 level teaspoons of sugar and stir well. Cover with polythene sealed with an elastic band. Each day for the next seven days feed the plant with one level teaspoon of sugar and one level teaspoon of ground ginger. Finally, on the ninth day, strain the mixture through some fine muslin and add a drop of lemon juice to the liquid.

Keep the sediment that remains after straining and divide it into two equal sized amounts. Place each half into separate clean jars and add half a pint of water, two level teaspoons of sugar and two level teaspoons of ground ginger. Continue as before for the next seven days.

The ginger beer can now be made either as a sweet still drink or as a dry sparkling ginger beer.

(Please note that it is most important to follow the recipes precisely so that there is no risk of bursting bottles or flying glass!)

Sweet Still Ginger Beer

Your prepared ginger beer plant
1lb sugar
1 pint boiling water

Place all the ingredients into a saucepan, stirring well until all the sugar has dissolved. Bring to the boil and simmer for five minutes to make sure that all the yeast has been killed. Then make it up to one gallon with cold water and bottle, corking it tightly and keep it for a few days before drinking.

Dry Sparkling Ginger Beer

Your prepared ginger beer plant
2oz sugar
1 gallon water

Add the sugar to the ginger beer plant and make it up to one gallon with the cold water, stirring all the time until all the sugar has dissolved. Bottle it into screw-top cider, beer, cordial or lemonade bottles and ensure that the tops are firmly secured. Keep it stored for seven to ten days, after which time the ginger beer should be sparkling and ready to drink.

Beer

To make a good and safe beer all the brewing equipment must be sterilised before every usage. This is extremely important! If you are unable to boil any of the utensils, wash them firstly with detergent or sterilising solution and rinse them using cold tap water. Next rinse them with a Sodium Metabisulphite solution followed by several rinses with cold tap water. (Also please note that if your water supply has been chlorinated it should be boiled and allowed to cool before any final rinses).

Honey Harvest Beer

½ oz hops
8oz honey or sugar
1 gallon cold water
1 tsp dried yeast or 1 tbsp brewer's yeast

Boil the hops and the honey (or sugar) in a large saucepan for approximately one hour with as much of the water as possible. Strain it into a plastic bucket and add more water to make it up to one gallon. Cool to 70°F/32°C. Add the yeast or float the brewer's yeast on a piece of toast. Cover it and leave it in a warm place for about forty eight hours. Siphon off into bottles, ensuring not to disturb the yeast deposit. Store it in a cool place for one week after which it will be ready to drink. The corks should be tied down if the beer is to be kept for any longer than just one week.

Mild Beer

(Original gravity - 1038)

2½lb malt extract
1lb dark dried malt extract
½ lb crystal malt
4oz roasted barley or black malt
1lb soft brown sugar
2oz Fuggles hops
4 gallons water
Top fermenting beer yeast
Caster sugar for priming the bottles

Boil the ingredients in at least one gallon of water, ensuring that the sugar does not stick. Strain it into a fermenting vessel through some fine muslin and then wash the grains and hops by pouring through with water, preferably using water that has been boiled first, until the volume in the fermenting vessel reaches four gallons. When cool (below 70°F/32°C), pitch with a top brewing beer yeast and cover it with a lid to exclude any flies, dust and bacteria etc. Allow it to ferment for four to five days at room temperature, skimming off the froth from the surface after two days. Skim again a second time and rack it (siphon off the liquid, leaving the sediment behind) into closed containers that are fitted with an airlock. Allow it to stand for a further seven to ten days for the fermenting to finish and allow all the yeast to sink to the bottom. Bottle it into beer bottles, priming each half pint bottle with a quarter teaspoon of caster sugar. Fit crown corks to ensure that the bottles are firmly sealed. Leave it to stand at room temperature for seven days and then leave it in a cool place to mature for a further fourteen days. This amount should make four gallons of mild beer.

Light Bitter Beer
(Original Gravity - 1032)

3lb malt extract
1lb crystal malt
1lb glucose chippings
3oz hops (perhaps 1½oz of Golding type and 1½oz of Fuggles)
4 gallons water
Top fermenting beer yeast
Caster sugar for priming

The method for brewing a light bitter beer is exactly the same as for the previous mild beer.

Export Pale Ale

4 gallons water
6oz crushed pale malt
4oz crushed crystal malt
4oz flaked maize
4oz wheat flour
3oz Goldings hops
9oz glucose chippings
4oz soft brown sugar
Carragheen Irish moss (for the appropriate quantities see manufacturer's instructions)
Top fermenting beer yeast
Caster sugar for priming the bottles
Water treatment (if required): a proprietary mixture of 1 tsp of gypsum, 1 tsp of epsom salts and 1 tsp of salt

Heat two and a half gallons of water to 165°F/74°C. Dissolve the water treatment, if used, into the hot water. Add the crushed pale malt, crushed crystal malt, flaked maize and wheat flour. Blending the wheat flour with a little cold water until creamy before adding will help to avoid lumps. The temperature will now have dropped to approximately 150°F/65°C, and this temperature should be maintained to aid the saccharification of the starch. After two hours strain the wort (the sweet liquid) off the grain and then wash the grains with water at 170°F/77°C until the total volume reaches four gallons.

Return all the liquid to the boiler and bring to the boil until all the frothing stops and then add the hops, glucose chips and the soft brown sugar. Boil it for one and a half hours, adding the Carragheen Irish moss just ten minutes from the end of the boiling time. After the full one and a half hours, turn off the heat. The volume should now have been reduced to approximately three gallons. Allow the hops to sink to the bottom of the boiler and let the liquid cool to 180°F/82°C. Then siphon it off into a fermenting vessel. Make up the wort in the fermenting vessel back to four gallons and cool it rapidly to bring the temperature down to 70°F/21°C. Now pitch the yeast and skim after twelve hours and stir. Leave it to stand at room temperature for five days or until a hydrometer reading reaches a gravity of ten. At this point skim off the yeast head and siphon into one gallon jars fitted with corks and airlocks. Leave it for a further seven days and then bottle it, priming each bottle with half a teaspoon of caster sugar to each pint bottle. Keep it in a warm place for one week and store it in a cool location for at least another six weeks.

Stout (The Yeast)

The following ingredients will produce two gallons of stout.

First make your yeast starter as follows at least twenty four hours before starting the main brew.

Yeast starter:

6fl oz water
1 dessertspoon malt extract
1 dessertspoon sugar
¼ tsp citric acid
Stout yeast

Add the malt extract, sugar and citric acid to the water. Bring it to the boil and allow it to boil for fifteen minutes. Cool it as quickly as possible and then pour it into a sterilised ten ounce (half pint) bottle. Plug the neck with a wad of cotton wool, cool it to below 70°F/20°C and then add the yeast. Replace the cotton wool plug and leave it in a warm place. The yeast should be fermenting vigorously in forty eight hours when the stout can be made.

(The yeast can be either a liquid culture or tablets. If a liquid culture is being used, shake the container well and add the contents to the cooled malt solution. Tablets can be added directly into the solution).

Stout (The Main Brew)

1½lb dried malt extract
8oz barley syrup
5oz roasted barley
3oz soluble dextrin
2oz Fuggles hops
2 gallons water
Caster sugar for priming the bottles

Boil all the stout ingredients together in water for at least one hour. Strain them through muslin into a sterilised fermenting vessel. Make the amount up to two gallons with cold boiled water and allow it to cool to below 70°F/21°C. Add the activated yeast and cover it loosely, letting the mixture ferment for five days at room temperature and skimming off the froth from the top as necessary. Siphon it into sterilised gallon jars, fit airlocks and let the stout ferment for about ten days, then siphon it off into beer bottles, priming each half pint bottle with a quarter teaspoon of caster sugar. Leave it to stand at room temperature for about a week and then store it in a cool place for at least another four weeks.

(This stout can also be used for making Christmas Puddings some two to three weeks before it is ready to drink.)

Lager (The Yeast)

First make a lager yeast starter as follows at least forty eight hours before you plan to brew the lager.

Yeast Starter

6fl oz water
1 dessertspoon malt extract
1 dessertspoon malt sugar,
¼ tsp citric acid
Lager yeast (either as liquid culture, tablets or granules)

Add the malt extract, sugar and citric acid to the water. Bring the mixture to the boil and continue boiling it for fifteen minutes. Cool it as rapidly as possible and then pour the mixture into a clean sterilised ten ounce (half pint) bottle. Plug the neck of the bottle with a wad of cotton wool and cool it right down to below 70°F/20°C. If you are using a liquid yeast culture, shake the phial and add the contents to the sterile malt liquid. Replace the cotton wool and keep it in a warm place. Tablet or granular form yeast is placed directly into the malt liquor. After forty-eight hours the yeast should be fermenting vigorously.

Lager (The Main Brew)

1½lb light dried malt extract
1lb brewing sugar or white invert sugar
1oz Hallertaver hops
½ tsp of ground Irish moss
Lager yeast starter
Water.
Campden powder or tablets
Caster sugar for priming the bottles

Boil all the ingredients excluding the yeast mixture and the Irish moss in one and a half gallons of water for one hour, ensuring that the malt and sugar do not stick. Fifteen minutes before the end of the boiling time add the Irish moss. Continue boiling for the remaining fifteen minutes and then strain the mixture though a muslin cloth into a sterile fermenting vessel. Wash the hops etc. with cold boiled water until the liquid volume reaches two gallons. Allow it to cool to below 70°F/20°C and then add the active yeast culture and stir well. Cover the brew and allow it to ferment in the fermenting vessel for five days, skimming off the froth after twenty four hours. After five days, skim off the surface once again and then siphon the brew into two one gallon jars with airlocks. Leave it for another ten days to allow the fermentation process to finish and the yeast to settle. Bottle it into beer bottles, priming each bottle with a quarter teaspoon of caster sugar per half pint bottle. Leave it to stand at room temperature for seven days and then place it in a cool place to clear and condition. This should take about six weeks.

If a plastic two gallon barrel is available the beer can be stored in bulk. To prime the barrel dissolve two and a half ounces of caster sugar in a little water and pour it into the barrel. Siphon in the brew and fix the bung securely. Store it at room temperature for a week and then relocate it to a cool place to mature. This will take approximately six weeks.

Old Strong Ale

This beer which has a starting gravity of approximately 1.078 will give an alcohol content of about 9% and it must therefore be sipped respectfully rather than quaffed. You have been warned!

3 gallons water
6lb crushed pale malt
6lb crushed crystal malt
1lb flaked barley
1lb barley, maize or wheat syrup
1lb glucose chippings
9oz soluble dextrin
12oz soft brown sugar
1oz Kent Golding hops
1oz Northern Brewer's hops
½ oz Bullion hops
General purpose yeast
Caster sugar for priming the bottles

Heat two gallons of water to 165°F/75°C. Mix in the pale malt, the crystal malt and the flaked barley. The temperature should now have dropped to about 150°F/62°C and this temperature must be maintained for one and a half hours. Strain out the sweet wort and wash the grains with water at 170°F/75°C until the total amount is three gallons. Bring the three gallons to the boil and allow it to boil very vigorously for half an hour. Add all the remaining ingredients except for the yeast and boil them vigorously for a further hour. Strain out the hops, bring it back up to three gallons with boiled water and then cool it down as quickly as possible. When the temperature has dropped to below 70°F/21°C, add the yeast and allow it to ferment for seven days in a fermenting vessel which must remain covered at all times. Then siphon it into gallon jars, fit airlocks and allow all the fermentation to complete its course. Next bottle it using half pint bottles with each one being primed with a quarter teaspoon of caster sugar. Cork the bottles very securely and store them away for at least three months before even attempting to drink it.

Wassail

6 cooking apples
Soft brown sugar
½ oz ground ginger
½ a grated nutmeg
A pinch of powdered cinnamon
8oz Demerara sugar
3 pints mild or brown ale
½ bottle raisin wine or ¼ bottle sherry
One lemon
10 lumps of sugar

Core the apples without peeling them. Fill in the hole with soft brown sugar and bake them in the oven (325°F/160°C/Gas mark 3) for 45 minutes to one hour, ensuring that they do not burst. Meanwhile, mix the ginger, nutmeg, cinnamon and Demerara sugar together in a saucepan. Add one pint of the ale and bring it to the boil. Stir in the rest of the ale, the wine and ten lumps of sugar that have been rubbed on the rind of the lemon. Reheat the mixture, but do not allow it to boil.

Place the roasted apples in a large bowl and pour on the hot ale mixture together with half the peeled, sliced lemon.

Wine Yeast Starter

Before starting out on any successful wine making process, the yeast should already be actively working as and when it is needed.

½ pint cold boiled water
1 level tbsp light dried malt extract
1 tsp sugar
½ tsp of either tartaric, malic, or citric acid
½ tsp yeast nutrient
Yeast (as recommended in the recipe)

Mix all the ingredients, stirring well until everything is fully dissolved. Pour into a sterilised bottle and seal the top with a cotton wool plug. Leave at a reasonably constant temperature (ideally 60-70°F/16-21°C) until working actively.

Yeast Starter

This starter is suitable for most wines and meads. It is best made at least forty eight hours before the wines and meads are started.

6fl oz water
1 dessertspoon malt extract
1 dessertspoon sugar
¼ tsp citric acid
Yeast (as recommended in the recipe)

Place the water, malt extract, sugar and citric acid in a saucepan and bring to the boil. Simmer for fifteen minutes, then cool it as swiftly as possible and pour it into a ten ounce (half pint) bottle. Plug the neck of the bottle with a cotton wool plug and cool it to below 70°F. If using a liquid yeast culture, shake well and add it to the cool malt liquor. Yeast in tablet form can be put straight into the cooled liquor. Replace the cotton wood plug and store in a cool place. The yeast should be fermenting well and vigorously within forty eight hours when you should be ready to start the wine making.

Barley Wine
(Original Gravity - 1085)

2½lb malt extract
1lb crystal malt
1½oz roasted barley or chocolate malt
1lb glucose chippings
1½lb soft brown sugar
4oz soluble dextrin (or glucose polymer)
2½oz hops
4 gallons water
Top fermenting beer yeast
General purpose yeast

Boil all the ingredients, except for the yeasts, in two gallons of water for at least one hour, ensuring that the glucose chippings and sugar do not stick. Strain into a fermentation vessel through some thin muslin and wash the grains and hops with cold boiled water until the liquor reaches two gallons. Allow it to cool and when the temperature is below 70°F/21°C, take out half a gallon and pitch this with the general purpose yeast, adding the top fermenting yeast to the other one and a half gallons. Now cover both brews and ferment for five days at room temperature. Skim the froth from the top after twenty four hours and again after five days. Then blend both fermenting liquids together and rack off into two one gallon jars and fit airlocks. Keep them at room temperature, allowing the fermentation to continue until it stops naturally which can take up to six weeks. Do not bottle your beer while it is still fermentating! When you are sure that all the fermentation has ceased, bottle it in 'Nip' sized or traditional small beer bottles using no priming sugar. Store it for at least six months and drink it with great caution. This beer will be EXTREMELY POTENT!!!!

Mulled Wine

A pinch of nutmeg
3 tbsp brown sugar
The juice and rind of either an orange or a lemon
1 cinnamon stick,
3 cloves
½ pint hot water
One bottle dry red wine (blackberry or elderberry if home-made, or any cheap red wine if purchased)

Simmer all the ingredients, except for the wine, for twenty minutes. Then add the wine. Reheat it but do not allow the mixture to boil. Serve it at once in thick glasses.

Hock Type Gooseberry Wine

Water
2 tbsp light dried malt extract
2lb sugar
¼ oz tartaric acid
¼ oz malic acid
¼ oz citric acid
Yeast energiser or nutrient*
Grape tannin*
Pectin reducing enzyme*
2lb hard green gooseberries
Hock, champagne or general purpose yeast
5 Campden tablets

(The * symbol used simply denotes that for the appropriate amounts please refer to the manufacturer's instructions)

Forty eight hours before you begin to make the wine, prepare a wine yeast starter using one of the suggested yeasts. Details of these are given on both Pages 7 and 8.

Bring about six pints or so of cold water to the boil, then remove from the heat and allow it to cool down. When cool, pour it into a sterilised plastic bucket and dissolve into it all the ingredients, except for the gooseberries, yeast and Campden tablets. Stir it well to ensure that everything has been dissolved and allow the mixture to cool. When cold, aerate the mixture by pouring the liquid back and forth from one to another sterilised vessel, finally finishing up with it in the original plastic bucket.

Wash the gooseberries well, preferably in sulphited water (3 Campden tablets in one gallon of water). Cut them in half and drop them into the now cold mixture in the plastic bucket. Finally, add the yeast starter. Stir it all together well, cover tightly and allow it to ferment for twenty four to thirty six hours. After the fermentation, strain the liquid away from the pulp into a sterilised gallon glass fermenting jar (a piece of fine muslin is ideal for this job), but do not squeeze the liquid through. Top it up to one gallon with cold boiled water, fit an airlock and let the fermentation proceed to dryness at a fairly constant temperature of 60-70°F/16-21°C. This should take from three to four weeks, the actual time depending on both the temperature and the care with which the must has been prepared. When the fermentation is complete, siphon it off into another sterilised gallon jar, taking care to avoid introducing any air into the wine. Top up the jar with any similar wine or cold boiled water. Add one Campden tablet, fix the airlock and set it aside in a cool dark place to clarify, which should take about five to six weeks. Siphon off the lees (dead yeast left at the bottom of the jar), top up the jar, add one further Campen tablet and then cork the jar extremely tightly. Leave it to stand for a further month before bottling and drinking.

Bilberry Wine
(as a dry red wine)

1 large (2lb 2oz) jar of bilberries in syrup (If using fresh or frozen bilberries, allow 1lb plus an extra five ounces of sugar in place of the syrup in the jar)
9-10fl oz red grape substitute
1½lb sugar
1 3mg Vitamin B1 tablet
Yeast nutrient and pectin reducing enzyme
Active yeast starter using general purpose wine yeast
Campden tablets
Cold boiled water

(As A Sweet Dessert Wine)

1 large (2lb 2oz) jar of bilberries in syrup (or fresh or frozen as suggested above)
1½lb or 18fl oz red grape concentrate
2lb 6oz sugar
3 3mg Vitamin B1 tablets
Yeast nutrient and pectin reducing enzyme
Active yeast starter using general purpose wine yeast
Campden tablets
Cold boiled water

Three to four days before making the wine, prepare the yeast starter following the directions given on page 7. If the fruit is fresh, frozen or dried, rinse it well using sulphited solution (3 Campden Tablets to one gallon of water) to kill off any wild yeasts and to clean the fruit. Rinse it off several times using fresh cold boiled water. Make sure you have to hand at least six pints of fresh cold boiled water.

Put the fruit in syrup (or the washed fruit) and the grape concentrate into a fermenting bucket. Dilute them with about two pints of cold boiled water. (If using fresh, frozen or dried bilberries, the additional five ounces of sugar should be made into a syrup using less than half a pint of cold boiled water and added to the fruit). Also add the vitamin B1 tablet/tablets, yeast nutrient, pectin reducing enzyme and yeast starter. Cover tightly and leave in a warm place to ferment for about thirty six hours.

Strain it off through a fine mesh or a sterilised muslin cloth to separate the fruit and pour the liquid into a one gallon glass fermenting Jar.

As a dry red wine

Mix up a syrup using the all the sugar and three pints of cold boiled water.

As A Sweet Dessert Wine

Mix up a syrup using one and a half pounds of the sugar and three pints of cold boiled water.

Mix one of these syrups (depending on the type of wine) into the contents of the glass fermenting jar, shake it well and then make it up to seven pints using cold boiled water. Fit an airlock and stand it in a warm place to ferment. The fermenting must will form a sticky head, but because the jar is not full it will not percolate through the airlock.

As A Dry Red Wine

When after a few days the frothing head has subsided, add the balance of cold boiled water, making the contents of the fermenting jar up to about one gallon. Leave it to ferment right out which should take no longer than three weeks at the most.

As A Sweet Dessert wine

When after a few days the frothing head has subsided, gradually make up the contents of the fermenting jar with syrup made up from the remaining sugar and cold water. This syrup must be added with care to the fermenting must, adding only a little at a time as there is often a lot of frothing involved that can spill out over the top if too much is put in at once. Finally cork it with an airlock and leave it in a warm place to ferment. This should take about three months.

Once the fermentation finishes, allow it to stand for a further week to allow most of the suspended matter to fall to the bottom.

The new raw wine will now be ready for racking. Siphon off the clear wine, leaving a deposit in the original jar that is totally untouched. Top up the jar with cold boiled water. Add one Campden tablet, fit an air lock and store it in a cool dark place to clear.

After a few weeks it should be clear. The wine should now be racked off again, following exactly the same method as used before. Do not forget to top up the jar again. Cork and leave it in a dark place for as long as possible.

When the time comes to drink this wine, siphon it all off into bottles which must be sealed with well fitted corks and stored in a dark place.

NOTE:-

When making dry red wine: after about two months there will be a definite increase in the quality. This will continue to improve for up to a year by which time the wine will be very good. Drink it within two years.

When making sweet dessert wine: if the wine is not sweet enough, then add some invert sugar just before drinking it at the rate of one to four ounces per bottle (according to taste). Dessert wines will probably take six months longer to mature than table wines to reach the equivalent quality. This particular wine will be very good if it is not drunk in the first year.

Elderflower Wine

Champagne yeast culture
Cold boiled water
1 pint fresh elderflowers
2 tbsp light dried malt extract
½ oz wine acid (a mixture of citric, malic and tartaric acids)
or the juice of two lemons
Yeast nutrient (using the quantity as stated by the manufacturer)
2lb sugar
Campden tablets

Forty-eight hours before commencing to make the wine, prepare the yeast starter using the champagne yeast culture. When making wine the best results are obtained by using liquid yeast cultures. Instructions on usage should come with the culture, but if not then follow the recipes on pages 7 or 8.

If possible choose white rather than cream coloured flowers. Pick them on a sunny and fine day. The flowers will deteriorate very quickly, making this a requirement. Lightly dry the flowers in the sun, if possible, to facilitate striping and shake each head vigorously to remove the maximum amount of pollen as too much pollen can make the wine go hazy.

Strip off all the petals into a suitable one pint measuring vessel. The taste of elderflowers is quite powerful and overdoing the measurement will not help unless you particularly want the extra flavour. Pour about six pints of cooled boiled water into a plastic bucket and dissolve into it the malt extract, wine acid (or lemon juice), the yeast nutrient and the sugar. Add the actively working yeast starter followed by the flowers. Stir it all well. Cover it tightly and leave it to stand for about forty eight hours to ferment. Stir it occasionally; three times a day should suffice.

After forty eight hours strain it off through some fine sterilised muslin and pour it into a one gallon glass fermenting jar. Top this up with cooled boiled water, fit an airlock and allow it to ferment until dryness. This will take about three weeks if the must has been properly prepared and the fermentation temperature maintained at 65-70°F/18-21°C.

When the fermentation has ceased, carefully rack off the lees into another sterilised one gallon jar, taking great care to minimise any contact with the air. Use a rubber tube to transfer it from one jar to another without splashing the wine, whilst leaving the sediment at the bottom of the first jar completely untouched. Top up the new jar to the top with cooled boiled water or with a similar wine if available. Add one Campden tablet and set it aside in a dark cool place to clarify.

In six weeks time the wine should be perfectly clear. Rack it off its lees once more, top up the jar, close the neck with a well fitted cork or lid and set it aside once again.
This wine should be quite dry to the taste, with little or no hint of sweetness. If tested with a hydrometer the reading should be below 1000.

If the wine does taste sweet and the hydrometer reading is well above 1000, or there has been any sign of slackening at an early stage, then do not proceed with the sparkling wine making with this batch. However, if all is well (and there is no reason why that should not be so if the wine has been made correctly and allowed to ferment at the proper temperature of 65-70°F/18-21°C) then it is at this stage that the wine is ready to be converted into a sparkling wine (see pages 49-53 for this process).

Gooseberry Wine

Champagne yeast culture
Cold boiled water
2 tbsp light dried malt extract
1lb 14oz sugar
½ oz wine acid (a mixture of citric, malic and tartaric acids)
¼ tsp grape tannin
Yeast nutrient (using the quantity as stated by the manufacturer)
Pectin reducing enzyme (using the quantity as stated by the manufacturer)
2lb hard green gooseberries
Campden tablets

Forty eight hours before commencing to make the wine, prepare a yeast starter using the yeast culture as described on page 7.

Bring six pints of cold tap water to the boil, remove it from the heat and allow it to cool down. When cool pour it into a sterilised plastic bucket and dissolve into it all the ingredients, except for the gooseberries, yeast and Campden tablets. Stir it well to ensure that everything has fully dissolved. Allow it to cool to room temperature. Next aerate the wine by pouring it back and forth from one to another sterilised bucket or vessel, but finally finishing up with it in the original plastic bucket.

Meanwhile, wash the gooseberries well, preferably in sulphited water (3 Campden tables in one gallon of water) and then rinse them well to remove any sulphite. Cut the gooseberries in half using a stainless steel knife and drop them into the now cold mixture in the plastic bucket. Finally add the yeast starter, stir well, seal tightly and set it aside to ferment for 36 hours.

After 36 hours strain off the pulp using a fine sterilised cloth, but do not squeeze the liquid through. Top up the liquid with cold boiled water until the one gallon mark is reached, fit an airlock and let the fermentation proceed at a constant temperature of 65-70°F/18-21°C. This can take up to four weeks, but should take no longer. The time taken will depend on the temperature and the care with which the must has been prepared.

When the fermentation has finished, carefully rack from the lees in to another sterilised gallon jar keeping any contact with the air to a minimum. Top up with a similar wine or cold boiled water. Add one Campden tablet, fit an airlock and set it aside in a cool dark place to clear. In five to six weeks the wine should be well clear, Rack it off once again from the lees, top up the jar and close up the neck with a well fitting cork or lid. Then set it aside.

To make this wine into a sparkling wine follow the instructions and directions on pages 49-53.

White Currant Wine

Champagne yeast culture
Cold boiled water
1½lb sugar
Yeast nutrient (¾ of the amount stated
by the manufacturer)
Pectin reducing enzyme (using the quantity as stated
by the manufacturer)
¼ oz malic acid (optional and for those who
prefer a high acid finish)
Campden tablets

The method used to make white currant wine is exactly the same as for gooseberry wine, but it is necessary to remove the stalks from the currants after washing and rinsing them. Then squeeze the fruit gently in order to burst the berries slightly. Do not pound them into a pulp, though.

When the fermentation has been completed, make it into a sparkling wine by following the directions on pages 49-53.

Apple Wine

The trouble with making apple wine is that there are so many different varieties and types of apple available, some of which are of poor quality, especially any of the 'seedling' types. Consequently you have to be far more specific about the apples to be used in the recipe. Cooking apples or eating apples on their own tend not to make the best wine. In proportion, about two thirds of the amount used should be eating apples (for flavour) and one third cooking apples (for crispness and freshness). This should give an ideal balance of flavours.

Champagne yeast culture
8lb prepared apples approx. (and not windfalls!)
1¼lb sugar
Pectin reducing enzyme (using the quantity as stated
by the manufacturer)
Yeast nutrient (using the quantity as stated
by the manufacturer)
¼ tsp grape tannin
Cold boiled water
Campden tables

NOTE!

An exact quantity of sugar cannot be given. The amount should be vatried in order to accommodate the sweetness (or lack of it) of the apples being used for the wine making. An ideal hydrometer reading should be 1080 when the juice and the sugar are added together. However, pulp fermentation makes this somewhat difficult as all apples contain some sugar. It is probably best, however, to err on the low side rather than on the high side.

Wash the apples well in sulphited water (3 Campden tables to a gallon of water). Remove any dirt, air pollution and all other foreign bodies. Rinse them well in clear cold tap water and inspect them all for any badly bruised or torn skin, hence the reason for not using windfalls. Bruised or broken skin usually results in infections which can lead to a poor tasting wine or even something akin to vinegar.

Put about four pints of previously boiled cold water into a sterilised plastic bucket. Add one crushed Campden tablet to this. Now crush the apples, or chop them into very small pieces using a stainless steel knife, and quickly drop the crushed or chopped apples into the cold water, submerging them completely to prevent any browning or change in flavour. When all the apples are in the bucket stir in the pectin enzyme, the yeast nutrient, the tannin and the actively working yeast starter (that was made at least two days beforehand). If possible, keep the apples completely submerged throughout the process by using a block of wood or some other non-toxic item. This can be a little difficult, but it is by no means impossible. It is worth the extra effort to keep the apples from the air, thus retaining both their natural colour and taste.

Each following day, on two or three occasions, squeeze the apples by hand. After two to three days they will have become quite soft and then they can be strained off.

Quickly separate the bulk of the apple pulp from the

juice by pouring everything through a plastic colander. Then strain it through a sterilised finely meshed cloth or muslin. Be sure to remove the maximum amount of solids from the juice. To the resulting liquid add the sugar, which should already have been dissolved in about two pints of cold water to make a syrup. Stir it well, pour it into a sterilised one gallon glass fermenting jar and top it up with cold boiled water. Cork it with an airlock and allow it to ferment to dryness at a constant temperature (ideally 65-70°F/18-21°C.). This should take no longer than three weeks, but the actual time taken will depend entirely on both the temperature and the care with which the must has been prepared.

Proceed from here on as for elderflower wine.

Making Sparkling Wines From Basic Wines

The wines to be used must be quite dry and should have finished working. They must also be totally clear before even attempting to make a sparkling wine.

It is most important that proper champagne bottles in good condition and without any scratches or any other defects are used. All such scratches and defects will weaken the structure of the bottles in much the same way as the scratch marks made by a glass cutter might weaken a pane of glass. Therefore great care must be taken when removing labels and any other ornamental signatures. If possible, use plastic implements to do this.

A further important factor when reusing champagne bottles is that when they are new they are made to withstand a pressure of 80lbs per square inch. It is certainly not advisable to build up to this kind of pressure when using second-hand bottles or with 'home-made expertise.' The syrup used in secondary fermentation gives some 40-43lbs per square inch, and this figure should never be exceeded.

You must use a proper method of sealing the bottles. You can easily get champagne type corks or stoppers from any good home-made wine suppliers.

Never ever attempt to make the wine stronger than the recipe because it will either not sparkle in the bottle, or alternatively it will sparkle too much, which may cause the bottles to explode.

Before a start is made, it is quite a good idea to decide where the bottles are to be stored for the duration of the secondary fermentation and maturation.

If you prefer to drink the wine without removing the sediment, store the bottles upright for the period of fermentation and maturation, but if you prefer to have the sediment removed, then I would suggest that you visit your local wine merchant and scrounge from him a couple of the strong cartons in which they receive their wines. You can then place yours bottled upside-down in them.

When basic wines requiring a long maturation are used to make sparkling wine, it is quite possible, and in fact might be preferable, to store the bottles on their sides. This, of course, can be done for all wines. When the time comes that they are ready to drink, stand them either upright or upside down as described above, but allow enough time for the lees or sediment to resettle before attempting to open the bottle.

To Make One Gallon Of Sparkling Wine

6 champange type bottles
6 plastic champagne type stoppers or corks
7 champagne type wires to secure the stoppers or corks.
1 gallon suitable wine, already tested for residual sugar and found to be satisfactory
6fl oz sugar syrup made from 1½oz of sugar dissolved in boiling water and allowed to cool.
6fl oz active yeast starter made using a liquid champagne yeast culture
Campden tablets

Forty eight hours before starting to make your sparkling wine, make up the yeast starter. Follow the directions given on page 7, but use only enough water to bring the volume of the starter up to six fluid ounces.

Soak the bottles overnight in a detergent solution, remove all the labels and then rinse out the insides of the bottles using a sulphited solution (2 Campden tablets per gallon of water) and then rinse the bottles under cold running water to remove all traces of sulphite.

Next assemble the six bottles on the floor beneath the one gallon jar of the selected wine. Carefully siphon the clear wine into the bottles, leaving sufficient room for the syrup and yeast (2fl oz.), plus also allowing for a good inch of air space. Now is the time to add in exact measurements one fluid ounce of the syrup and one fluid ounce of the yeast starter.

Drive home the champagne type stoppers and seal them

well using the champagne type wires, making sure that the wires engage the slots provided in the stoppers. Tighten the wires securely, making sure that they have fully engaged under the lip on the neck of the bottle.

Shake the bottles well so as to distribute the syrup uniformly throughout the contents of the bottle. Store them in a dark place with an ideal temperature of approximately 65°F/18°C either in a standing position, lying flat or upside down in a carton.

After a few weeks it should be possible to see if the yeast is doing its job properly by checking the wires around the tops of the bottles. They should now be visibly strained and the stopper itself should protrude somewhat and, on carefully lifting the bottles, a deposit, perhaps at this stage only slight, should be visible. If this is so then everything is going according to plan.

It is practically impossible to say just how long a period of time the process will take, but if six months passes with no apparent developments having taken place, then I would suggest that a bottle be opened to check. It is always possible that a failure could have developed through there perhaps being too much alcohol present in the basic starting wine or the yeast not being properly active.

When it is seen that the process described above has taken place, the bottles should be transferred to a cooler place to mature. A long maturation is not always desirable and usually the lighter the wine, the quicker it can be drunk, even if it has not been matured.

Sparkling wines based on the prceding elderflower,

gooseberry, white currant, and apple wines will be delicious if drunk as soon as the secondary fermentation has completely finished.

At this juncture it is perhaps useful to point out that the colder the wine is, the lower the pressure will be at the time of opening the bottle.

To Drink Wine Without Removing The Sediment

The bottles should all have been standing in an upright position so that the sediment has formed in the punt in the base of the bottle. To achieve the best result, place the bottle in a refrigerator without tilting it and cool it to as low a temperature as possible. Under no circumstances, however, should you use a domestic freezer for this purpose due to the possibility of the base of the bottle fracturing due to the cold.

Then, with one hand, carefully tip the bottle onto its side, taking great care not to disturb the sediment. Then point the stopper into the centre of a plastic bucket placed at 45°. Undo the wires with caution and, in all probability, the stopper will fly out gently into the bucket with only a slight frothing of the contents. You can then, with caution, pour the contents of the bottle into the waiting glasses without ever tipping the bottle back into an upright position which would, of course, disturb the sediment. If the glasses are cool too there will also be very little frothing in them, which should make for a good, straight pour.

To Drink Wine After Removing The Sediment

The bottles should have been stored in an upside-down position and this will have created a sediment build up in the hollow of the stopper. Without tipping the bottle from its upside-down position, place it in a refrigerator and cool it down to as low a temperature as possible. In this instance you can use a home freezer as, unlike with the previous task, it does not run the risk of damage to the base of the bottle as it is the stopper end at which the sediment has accumulated. Place the bottle, still upside down, suitably and safely propped up and leave it for about half an hour. During this time the sediment in the stopper will freeze up. Using gloves remove the bottle from the freezer and turn it slowly to a horizontal position. Cut or remove any wires and the stopper should fly out, or alternatively can be eased out gently, taking the sediment with it. The contents can then be poured into one or two glasses at a time.

Always store any sparkling wines in a cool dark place once they have completed their secondary fermentation and always serve them chilled.

Red wine can be made sparkling too, but it is far less popular than either white or rosé. This is possibly due to the extra tannin content of red wines.

Dry Sherry Type Wine

(to be made in early spring)

1 gallon birch sap
1lb sultanas (washed and either chopped or minced)
6oz dried bananas (washed and either chopped or minced)
2lb 10oz sugar
1 tsp tartaric acid
1 level tsp grape tannin
1 tsp yeast nutrient
¼ tsp yeast energiser
Sherry yeast in starter form
Polish spirit or vodka (to fortify the
wine after fermentation)
A few drops, per bottle, of sherry essence when bottling

Birch sap can be collected in early spring when the sap is rising in the trees and the buds have yet to burst into leaf. It is obtained by drilling a small, upwardly inclined hole about 1½ inches into the tree. It is best to drill the hole about two feet above the ground or the base of the trunk. A rubber or plastic tube the same size as the drill bit is then inserted into the hole and the sap allowed to drip into a gallon jar. Sap should only be taken from a mature tree with a girth of about ten inches and it is most important that a plug is knocked into the drill hole after the tapping is concluded in order to prevent further unnecessary bleeding that might harm the tree.

After collecting one gallon of birch sap it should be brought gently to the boil and allowed to simmer for fifteen minutes to ensure sterility. Then pour it onto the rinsed sultanas and bananas in a clean sterile bin. Stir in the sugar and continue stirring to ensure it is completely dissolved. When it has cooled down add the tartaric acid, tannin, nutrient, energiser and the sherry yeast. Allow it to ferment on the pulp for five days and then strain it off into a clean and sterile gallon fermenting jar and fit an airlock.

Let all the fermentation finish completely and then rack it off into another sterilised gallon jar, avoiding disturbing the lees. Refit the airlock.

After three months the wine should be clear. Rack it off again and fortify it to taste with Polish spirit or Vodka and the sherry essence.

The wine can now be bottled and it will continue to mature for several years in the bottles, but should be fit to drink after twelve months.

Blackberry And Apple Wine
(A red table wine)

5lb apples
3lb blackberries
1lb elderberries
8oz sultanas or raisins
4oz dried bananas
1 gallon water
Sugar to adjust the wine to a gravity of 1.090
Pectin enzyme (to be used as recommended
by the manufacturer)
1 tsp of yeast nutrient
¼ tsp of yeast energiser
Burgundy or Bordeaux yeast in starter form

Wash the apples, pulp them and squeeze out all of the juice. Pour the juice only into a sterile fermenting vessel. Wash the blackberries and elderberries, pulp them and add them to the apple juice. Wash and chop the sultanas and dried bananas and add them to the contents of the fermenting vessel. Finally make up the volume to one gallon using cold water.

When it is cold strain out enough juice to achieve a specific gravity reading and adjust the bulk using sugar to reach a specific gravity of 1.090. One pound of sugar dissolved in one gallon of water will raise the specific gravity by a figure of 37.

Stir in all the remaining ingredients and allow them to ferment for four days.

After this period strain it carefully into a sterile fermenting jar taking care not to squeeze the pulp and top it up with cold boiled water. Fit an airlock and ferment it out to dryness.

The final specific gravity should be .990 or lower.

Rack it off into another clean sterilised gallon jar, taking great care not to disturb the lees. Add one Campden tablet and refit the airlock.

Leave it to mature for at least twelve months, racking it off every four months if a deposit forms. The wine can then be bottled and left to mature for a further six months in the bottles.

Sweet Mead

2lb heather honey and 1lb clover honey
1 gallon water
1 tsp yeast nutrient
¼ tsp yeast energiser
1 3mg B1 tablet
½ oz malic acid
¼ oz tartaric acid
½ tsp grape tannin

Mead yeast is made up into a yeast starter with 8 ounces of Demerara sugar used for sweetening after fermentation.

Dissolve the honeys in two pints of water and heat the temperature to 40°F/60°C. Maintain this temperature for at least half an hour to pasteurise the honeys. All honeys are high in wild yeasts, bacteria and moulds etc. which must be destroyed before any fermentation can take place or strange and unusual flavours could possibly develop in the mead.

After the pasteurisation process pour the honeys into a clean and sterile fermenting bucket, making it up to one gallon with cold boiled water. Cover the bucket securely and when it is cold add all the remaining ingredients except for the Demerara sugar and allow it to ferment for five days.

After five days transfer it by siphoning into a clean sterilised gallon jar, making it up to one gallon with cold boiled water and keep it at a constant temperature of 75°F/25°C and sealed with an airlock until all fermentation has finished.

Now dissolve the Demerara Sugar in as small an amount of water as possible, heat it to boiling point and allow it to boil gently for ten minutes. Then cool down the sugar solution as quickly as possible and pour it into a clean sterilised gallon jar and siphon the mead onto it without disturbing the lees in the bottom of the first jar.

If the freshly racked liquid does not fill the gallon jar, top it up with cold boiled water to the one gallon mark, sealing the vessel with an airlock again.

The mead should be racked every four months if a heavy deposit continues to form at the bottom and topped up again with cold boiled water. It is possible that it will take up to two years or more for your mead to become 'star bright,' but mead should be matured for a long period, possibly up to four years when using Heather Honey.

Please note that you could use other floral honeys, but it is best to avoid Australian honeys as they may contain eucalyptus.

Sweet Orange Wine

First make a yeast starter at least forty eight hours before beginning production of this wine.

The Yeast Starter

6fl oz water
1 dessertspoon malt extract
1 dessertspoon sugar
¼ tsp citric acid
Sauterne yeast

Put the water, malt extract, sugar and citric acid into a pan and bring them to the boil. Allow the ingredients to boil gently for fifteen minutes. Cool the solution as quickly as possible and then pour it into a sterilised ten ounce (half pint) bottle. Plug the neck with a wad of cotton wool and cool it to below 70°F/21°C. Add the yeast, reseal the bottle and leave it in a warm place.. The Yeast should be fermenting well within about forty eight hours when production of the main wine can be started

The Wine

4lb oranges
1lb raisins
3lb sugar
1 tsp yeast nutrient
½ tsp yeast energiser
A pinch of grape tannin
Two Wheetabix or Shredded Wheat
Cold boiled water
Campden tablet

Wash the oranges, squeeze them and place the juice in a sterile plastic bucket. Take the skins of half of the oranges, remove the pith and roast them in a medium oven for about 25-30 minutes or until they become crisp and brown.

Wash and chop the raisins and add them to the juice. Now add the roasted skins, sugar, yeast starter, yeast nutrient, yeast energiser, tannin and either the Weetabix or Shredded Wheat, adding cold boiled water to bring the volume up to a gallon. Cover the fermenting bucket lightly and ferment on the pulp for forty eight hours at room temperature, stirring twice daily.

Strain everything carefully into a clean sterilised gallon fermentation jar, fit an airlock and leave it to stand at room temperature to allow the fermentation process to completely finish, topping up the jar to the one gallon mark with cold boiled water after seven days, if necessary. Fermentation can take up to eight weeks depending on both the weather and the temperature.

When all the fermentation is completed, rack the wine into another clean sterile jar taking great care to avoid disturbing the lees.

Add one Campden tablet and top it up to the one gallon mark with either cold boiled water or with sugar syrup if you decide that the wine is not quite sweet enough.

Leave it to stand until it is brilliantly clear, racking it off again after four months if a heavy deposit forms. Leave it to mature for at least nine months after which the wine will be ready for bottling and also ready to drink.

Parsnip Wine

4lb parsnips
3lb sugar
1 gallon water
Some lemons or citric acid
Yeast

Cut the parsnips up into small pieces and boil them, but do not allow them to get too soft. They should be just 'prickable' using an ordinary fork. You can boil a couple of lemons with them too if you have them to hand. Strain off the liquor and stir in the sugar while hot so as to melt it. Some people also like raisins in the wine. If that includes you then add a few now and also some citric acid or liquid lemon juice and ferment it with the yeast as soon as the temperature has cooled to below blood heat (98.4°F/35°C) before putting in the yeast. Allow it to ferment in gallon fermination jars fitted with airlock corks.

Rack it off into a clean one gallon fermination jar using fresh cold boiled water to bring it up to the gallon mark. Refit the air lock cork and store it in a cool dark place for at least two years.

Rhubarb Wine

15lb rhubarb
2½lb sugar
1gallon water
Yeast

Chop up the rhubarb and place it in a clean sterile plastic brewing bucket. Add the boiling water and mash up the rhubarb. Leave it to soak overnight, strain off all the liquid and press the fruit to get as much of the juice as possible. Stir in the sugar until it is all dissolved and sprinkle in the yeast. When the fermentation is finished, decant it off into a one gallon jar with an airlock for two weeks and then bottle it. Store it in a cool dark place for six weeks. The wine should then be ready to drink.

Elderberry Wine

4lb elderberries
3lb sugar,
1 gallon water
Yeast.

Remove the berries from their stalks. Place them in a plastic fermination bucket and pour on the boiling water. Mash the berries well, cover them and leave to soak for twenty four hours. Add the yeast, cover once more and allow it all to ferment. When the fermenation has finished rack it off into a one gallon fermentation jar with an airlock and seal well. Store it in a cool dark place and allow the wine to mature for about three months. It should then be very drinkable.

Dandelion Wine

3 quarts (2 pints) dandelion heads
1 large lemon
3lb sugar
2 oranges
1 gallon water
Yeast

Remove as much of the green calyxes from the flowers as possible. You may find gloves to be useful while doing this job. Put the flowers into a clean sterile fermenting bucket, pour the gallon of boiling water over them and cover and leave them for three days, stirring several times. Pour into a preserving pan and bring to the boil with the thin peel from all the fruit.. Allow it to simmer for ten minutes and then strain it over the sugar, stirring well to dissolve it all. When it is luke warm add the juices of the oranges and lemon to the previously prepared yeast. Pour it into a one gallon demijohn (fermentation jar), fit it with an airlock and allow it to ferment till finished. Bottle it up leaving any sediment behind. Store it in a cool dark place for at least a month, by which time it should be ready to drink.

Nettle Wine

2 quarts young nettle tops (usually a standard
bucket full, but not pressed down)
1 large lemon
3lb sugar
Yeast
1gallon water

Wash the nettles well using rubber gloves. Simmer them with the gallon of water and the thinly peeled lemon rind for about forty five minutes. Strain the liqour on to the sugar, stiring well until all the sugar has dissolved.   When it has cooled to luke warm, add the prepared yeast and the juice of the lemon. Cover and leave it in a fermenting vessel for about a week. This wine usually gives a fierce fermentation at first and it can and probably will boil over and make a fine mess for you to clear up if put into a demijohn too soon, so let it calm down a little in the bucket.   After about a week, bottle it up and keep in a cool dark place. It should be drinkable after about a month to six weeks.

Gorse Wine

1 gallon gorse flowers
2 oranges
3lb sugar
One1 large or two small lemons
1 gallon water
Yeast

Simmer the flowers and thinly peeled lemon rinds for fifteen minutes. Strain them out onto the sugar, and stir well until all the sugar has dissolved. Pour it into a one gallon demijohn sealed with an airlock together with the yeast and allow it to ferment until the process is complete.

Bottle it when all fermentation has finished. Store it in a cool dark place to mature for about four weeks.

May Blossom Wine

2 pints mayblossom
1 orange
3lb sugar
1 lemon
1 gallon water
Yeast

Boil the water with the sugar and fruit peel and allow it to simmer for fifteen minutes. Put the flowers into a sterile plastic wine making bucket and pour over the hot liquid. When it has cooled to luke warm, add the yeast. Leave the mixture in the fermentation vessel for three days, remembering to stir the wort twice a day. Strain it into a one gallon demijohn, fit an airlock and allow it to ferment completely. Bottle it up leaving any sediment in the bottom of the demijohn.

Store it in a cool dark place to mature.

Blackberry Wine

3lb blackberries
2½lb sugar
Wine yeast
Pectin destroying enzyme
1 gallon water

Crush the blackberries thoroughly with a spoon in a sterilized bucket and cover with a full kettle of boiling water.

Cover and leave them for twenty four hours. Strain off the liqour and bring it up to one gallon using cold tap water. Add the sugar and stir well to dissolve. Add the Pectin destroying enzyme with the wine yeast.

Cover once again and leave it in a warm dry place to ferment. After about a week or so, the fermentation will subside. Gently stir and pour it into a gallon fermentation jar fitted with an airlock. Leave it to finish fermenting in a cool dark place. When all the fermentation has finished, after two months or so, carefully syphon off the liquor into a fresh clean sterilized jar, leaving the sediment behind.   Top up this new jar to one gallon using cooled boiled water and refit an airlock. Leave it to mature in a cool dark place before bottling after six months.

Pea-Pod Wine

5lb pea-pods (or whatever you have)
½ lb sultanas
1¾lb sugar
Pectin destroying enzyme
Wine yeast
1 cup black tea
¼ tsp citric acid
½ tsp malic acid

Mince or liquidise the sultanas, add them to the pea-pods together with four pints of water and simmer for thirty minutes. Strain off the liquor on to the sugar stirring well to dissolve it all and then allow it to cool. Add all the other ingredients and bring it up to one gallon using tap water. Cork it with an airlock and leave it to ferment in a cool dark place.

Then follow the recipe as for blackberry wine.

Rose Wine

5 pints red rose flower petals (lightly pressed
down in a measuring jug)
½ lb sultanas
2lb sugar
Pectin destroying enzyme
White yeast
1 cup black tea
¼ tsp citric acid
½ tsp malic acid
½ tsp tartaric acid

Pour three pints of boiling water over the petals and minced sultanas. Cover and leave it to soak for twenty four hours. Strain off the liquid and add all the other ingredients, Cover and leave it to ferment in a warm place. Then proceed as for blackberry wine through to bottling, but protect the wine from direct light if red petals have been used.

Most other flower wines can be made in precisely this fashion.

Pressed Apple Wine

1 gallon pressed apple juice
2-2½lb sugar (according to taste)
Pectin destroying enzyme
Wine yeast

Press the apples to get the apple juice, Add the sugar and pectin destroying enzyme and stir to dissolve them thoroughly, Add the wine yeast, cover and leave to ferment, proceeding as for the previous recipes up to bottling.

A mix of apples such as sweet eaters, cooking apples and if possible some cider apples are really needed to achieve the correct wine balance.

If you do not have an apple press you can chop up the apples as small as possible and cover them with cold water in a sterilized vessel, Use as much fruit as the water will cover. Add the wine yeast, cover and then set it aside for a week, stirring vigorously twice daily. Strain off the liquid and squeeze as much juice from the pulp as possible using a muslin cloth. Stir in the sugar according to taste and the pectin destroying enzyme thoroughly and transfer to a demijohn with an airlock. Proceed as with previous recipes through to bottling.

This yields a wine lighter in colour and flavour than from pressed apples, but it is still well worth making.

Sloe Gin

2lb sloes
4 pints gin or juniper flavoured spirit
8oz sugar

Freeze the sloes for twenty four hours and then defrost them.

Place the split sloes, sugar and gin into big wide necked vessels with screw-topped lids. Screw the tops down tightly and shake the jars vigourously. Shake them every few days for the next three months. Strain the liquor off off through muslin and decant it into smart bottles and label them.

This sloe gin will be ready to drink for Christmas provided that it is made as soon as the sloes are available, but it will improve greatly with keeping like many other liquors.

Do not discard the gin soaked sloes. Simply remove the stones, chop them finely and you will end up with an instant topping for ice cream.

Sparkling Cider

If actual cider apples are not available, do not worry. Just try to get a good mix of dessert and cooking apples in the proportion of 60/40 and mix in a good ration of crab apples or apples with a degree of bitterness or astringency. If these are unavailable simply add a pinch of tannin from the wine maker's cabinet. Crush the juice out of the apples and fill the juice up to the neck of a vessel that can accomodate an airlock or perhaps a larger fermentation lock, but do not fit it yet. Add two level teaspoons of yeast with nutrients per each gallon of juice and plug the opening with a loose wad of cotton wool. When the fermentation quietens down after two or three days, remove the debris, wipe the neck with a clean piece of cotton wool and fit the fermentation lock.

Ferment it to dryness which can take anything from six weeks to three months depending on the temperature and apple varieties, or until the cider has nearly cleared and the bubbles ceased. This will mean a specific gravity of 1005 or less.

Rack it off, add six ounces of white sugar made up into a syrup to each gallon of racked young cider and move it to a warm place. Ferment it to dryness once again and rack off and move it to a cold place, still under an airlock for two weeks or at least until the cider is nearly clear. Now rack it off again, but allow a little of the deposited yeast to come through so that you are working with a slightly hazy but by no means cloudy cider.

For a dry sparkling cider add four level teaspoons of white sugar to each gallon of cider. Bottle it into bottles that are made to take considerable pressure. Store it in a cool dark place for two to three months to allow the cider to condition and develop. If you want to speed up the process in time to drink the cider at Christmas and the New Year, it is possible to bring the bottles into the warmth for a couple of weeks before returning them to a cool dark place.

For a medium sweet sparkling cider add white sugar syrup, dissolving it thoroughly in the cider until it is just sweet to the taste with a specific gravity of about 1012. Bottle it and treat it as above.

On no account should you sulphite or pasteurise your cider and always serve it very cold!

Making Country Wines, Ales & Cordials

The Good Life Press Ltd.
The Old Pigsties, Clifton Fields
Lytham Road, Preston
PR4 0XG
01772 633444

The Good Life Press Ltd. is a family run business specialising in publishing a wide range of titles for the smallholder, 'goodlifer' and farmer. We also publish Home Farmer, the monthly magazine for anyone who wants to grab a slice of the good life - whether they live in the country or the city.

A-Z of Companion Planting by Jayne Neville
A Guide to Traditional Pig Keeping by Carol Harris
Ben's Adventures in Wine Making by Ben Hardy
Building and Using Your Clay Oven by Mike Rutland
Build It! by Joe Jacobs
Build It!....With Pallets by Joe Jacobs
Craft Cider Making by Andrew Lea
Flowerpot Farming by Jayne Neville
Grow and Cook by Brian Tucker
Grow it Yourself by Gail Harland
Making Jams and Preserves by Diana Sutton
No Time To Grow by Tim Wootton
Precycle! by Paul Peacock
Raising Chickens by Mike Woolnough
Raising Goats by Felicity Stockwell
The Bread and Butter Book by Diana Sutton
The Frugal Life by Piper Terrett
The Medicine Garden by Rachel Corby
The Polytunnel Companion by Jayne Neville
The Sausage Book by Paul Peacock
The Sheep Book for Smallholders by Tim Tyne
The Smoking and Curing Book by Paul Peacock
Soap Craft by Diana Peacock
Urban Beekeeping by Craig Hughes
Woodburning by John Butterworth
Worms and Wormeries by Mike Woolnough

www.goodlifepress.co.uk
www.homefarmer.co.uk